A PIL(
IN
THE PULPIT

CW01336005

A selection of Sermons
Preached by
Reverend V Victor Cooper MA
Former Honorary Chaplain
Of the Aircrew Association

This selection is published by
The Aircrew Association Archive Trust
2003

1

Published by the Aircrew Association Archive Trust

Editor: Wing Commander Alan R Watkins BA FRSA RAF (Retd)
51 Townside, Haddenham, Aylesbury HP17 8AW
Tel: 01844 291275

First Impression October 2003

ISBN 0-9545963-0-7

Printed by: MPT Colour Graphics Ltd

Contents

Foreword

Photograph:

Foreword

This collection of sermons has been selected from more than twenty sermons which I have preached since I was invited to become the first Honorary Chaplain of the Aircrew Association. The sermons are presented unedited and in full – as they were preached.

They were preached at various places where the autumnal ACA Reunions were held and at St Clement Dane's church in London.

A few short passages appear in more than one sermon: this is due to the fact that the sermons were preached to differing congregations.

I have had many requests for copies of my sermons and I would like to thank sincerely Air Cdre Jack Broughton, Air Cdre Graham Pitchfork and Wg Cdr Alan Watkins for the help that they have given me in the production of this book and in the selection of its contents.

As an introduction to the anthology I will quote the reply which I made to Sir Michael Knight (then President of the ACA) when he inducted me to my office in St Clement Dane's Church.

V. Victor Cooper

V Victor Cooper

Reverend V Victor Cooper MA
Honorary Chaplain of the Aircrew Association

6

My Induction as Honorary Chaplain of The Aircrew Association

This is the text of my reply to Air Chief Marshal Sir Michael Knight KCB, AFC, FRAeS, President of the Aircrew Association when, in St. Clement Dane's Church on 28th April 1996, he inducted me to the position of Honorary Chaplain of the Aircrew Association and presented me with a clerical stole bearing the A.C.A. badge.

I would like to say to you, Sir Michael, and to the Aircrew Association as a whole: thank you. I assure you that I feel myself very highly honoured to be invested with this clerical stole as Chaplain of the ACA and I promise that I will do my best to be a worthy shepherd of the flock to which I have now been appointed.

What a flock!

Did ever anyone have a flock like it?

All wearing ribbons and medals and decorations as tokens of their great courage and representing innumerable acts of outstanding bravery;

And all of them able to tell such tales of "derring-do" as would rival the Rhyme of the Ancient Mariner.

So, it is a fairly daunting undertaking that lies before me.

These are not so much a flock of sheep - much more a pride of lions, even though I have noticed that some of these lions are showing a few silver threads among the gold of their manes - and when I remind myself that these people are my contemporaries, I am driven to the conclusion that I must soon be approaching the first stages of early middle-age myself!

So, it is with some trepidation that I take up my pastoral staff!

When I joined the Royal Air Force in May 1940 I was already an ordinand - but that was the time that Hitler and his chiefs-of-staff were looking across the Channel with envious eyes at our White Cliffs of Dover - through binoculars! I thought that very inappropriate - but that was a long time ago and happily - happily - things are very different now: and for that we thank God.

But I am proud to stand with the lads of the ACA - and I am proud to be their Chaplain, - and if, in any way, I can mediate to them something of the Grace of our Lord Jesus Christ, I shall be more than content.

Thank you.

In the Epistle to the Hebrews Chapter 11 and verse 13 we read: "These all died in faith not having received the promises, but having seen them, and greeted them from afar".

As he draws near to the end of his letter, the author of the Epistle to the Hebrews brings his argument to a conclusion by referring to the heroes of Hebrew history who had performed so many valiant deeds in the service of their people. He writes: "and what shall I more say, for the time would fail me to tell of Gideon, Barak, Samson, Jephthah, Samuel, and so many others .....".

He refers to their mighty exploits in Battle, their suffering under persecution, their deprivations, hardships and loneliness and finally, and most important, their Faith. The Faith they had in their people's future, The Faith which was their own strength and comfort, The Faith for which so many of them died. And he upholds them as a challenge to himself and to all those to whom he writes:

"These all died in faith, not having received the promises, but having seen them and greeted them from afar".

Today we remember those who lost their lives in war: The Great War; The Korean War; Northern Ireland; the Falklands; and in the war which we particularly remember because it profoundly affected all our lives - The Second World War - the war against Naziism.

How vividly those days of 50 years ago come back to us: how well we remember Churchill's speeches in 1940: "We will never surrender..... On land and sea and in the air we will fight this evil thing ... the Nazi regime.... whose wicked deeds are made more sinister by the lights of perverted science".

We had a long and costly way to go:

We remember Dunkirk and the Battle of Britain, D-Day, VE Day, VJ Day and the price we paid to get there.

We remember the soldiers who fought and died in France, North Africa, Italy, and Burma.

We remember those who were captured and died wretched deaths as prisoners of the Japanese.

We remember the thousands of sailors who have no known grave but the sea:

We remember the airmen who flew out on sorties and never returned;

We remember the women who died in all branches of the armed forces;

We remember the civilians who died in the streets or even in their own homes;

We remember the wounded, maimed, blinded, the broken in mind;

It is a truly appalling catalogue, and they were not just names. They were people: fathers, husbands, brothers, sons, daughters, and sweethearts.

To many people in Europe in the summer of 1940, when Great Britain and her empire allies stood alone, it must have seemed that evil had triumphed - it was everywhere victorious and what was the point of continuing to fight it? But on the continent there were many who would not accept this - and they organised Resistance Movements. They risked everything ~ in their struggle against Naziism. Think of the slow, slow hours of harrowing anxiety they faced; the fear of betrayal; the unspeakable fate which awaited them if arrested. How many of these paid with their lives for their brave defiance?

It would be very easy to draw up a modern version of that list of heroes' names that we have in the Epistle to the Hebrews. "These all died in faith"- in the faith that the cause they served was right; and must in God's good time prevail over the arrogant evil of the Nazi State.

And let us never forget this: that there were many Germans who felt that in Nazi Germany: people seldom mentioned, but who must never be forgotten for their faith and courage which was truly heroic. It is to the credit and the honour of Germany that so many did oppose, resist and denounce the evil ways of the Nazis and the dreaded Gestapo.

These people very soon found themselves in Concentration Camps. There was no great delay in the staging of their trials; and the trials themselves did not last long. They were sentenced to death as "enemies of the state" and died on the gallows or in front of firing squads.

But many of these fine brave people managed to write letters, which were smuggled out of the prisons in which they awaited their end - and a surprising number of these letters have survived.

One was written by Helmut James, Count Von Moltke (A relative of the famous German field-marshal). In January 1944 he discovered that one of his friends was about to be arrested by the Gestapo. He warned his friend and the friend escaped, but Helmut Von Moltke was arrested. In his last letter from prison he wrote:

"When I was taken into the court for my last words I was in such a frame of mind that I nearly said I have only one thing to add to my defence: Take my goods, my honour, my children and wife; the body they may kill; but GOD'S TRUTH abideth still - his kingdom is for ever!" But that would only have

9

made it harder for the others; Therefore I said only "I do not intend to say anything, Herr President." He was executed by firing squad in January 1945. He had saved his friend's life at the cost of his own.

Kurt Huber was a Professor at Munich University who could not hide his opposition to "National Socialism". He was arrested by the Gestapo in February 1943 and charged with "high treason". In his last statement before the court he said: "You have taken from me the status and the rights of a professor, as well as my doctorate attained "summa cum laude", and placed me on a footing with the lowest criminal. But no trial for "high treason" can rob me of the dignity of a university professor, or a man who openly and courageously avows his view of the world and the state. The inexorable course of history will vindicate my actions, and my purposes: On this I rely "with adamant faith". I hope in God's name that the spiritual forces that will vindicate them may be born in good time from my own nation. I have acted, as I had to act - in response to an inward voice; I accept the consequences… All my beloved ones! May Almighty God bless and take you into his care."

He was executed in July 1943

These all died in faith – "in ADAMANT FAITH".

Alfred Delp was a devout Roman Catholic who deplored the political wickedness of Germany - and said so. He was arrested in July 1944. In prison he wrote a number of letters. Let me read a few lines of his last one:

"So farewell, … my crime is that I had faith in Germany - a faith surmounting even a possible interim of desolation and darkness. That I did not believe in that insensate trinity of PRIDE, ARROGANCE and FORCE. … and that I did this as a Roman Catholic Christian and as a Jesuit. And so, in conclusion, I shall do what I have done so often before - but with fettered hands…..what I shall continue to do so long as I am permitted to breathe, I shall give blessing. I shall bless land and people; bless this beloved German nation in its distress and inner anguish. I shall bless the church that its sources, its springs, may flow within it once more purer and cleaner. As for myself, however, I intend to wait here faithfully for the dispensation and guidance of the Lord God. I shall trust in Him until they take me away."

They did. They hanged him in February 1945

Saint Paul was not the only person who wrote great letters from prison. And these letters - for all the agony and unhappiness that lies behind them - I find immensely inspiring. They reveal a nobility of the human spirit and unshakeable faith in the vindication of the GOOD. In their way these men were fighting for TRUTH and RIGHTEOUSNESS and MORAL GOODNESS to prevail.

What were we fighting for? Just to Win? To defeat the Nazis? For King and Country? For Democracy? For Liberty and Freedom? Could we go on: for Righteousness, Truth and Goodness?

Liberty and Freedom are not enough. We have Liberty and Freedom, preserved for us at that appalling cost. What are we doing with our FREEDOM?

Freedom can so easily degenerate into a progressive abandonment of all moral restraints. Freedom is not just a privilege - it carries heavy responsibility.

It is easy to confuse "Freedom" with "my being free to do just as I please".

In the Bible there is a verse which, with laconic brevity, simply says, "It is righteousness that exalteth a nation". (Proverbs 14 v 34)

It is moral goodness. In the war we were all sure that we were not only fighting to win – but fighting for the RIGHT. Moral and Spiritual values counted.

When we looked at what had happened in Germany we were determined that, in our schools, children should not be given a political brainwashing every morning, but have lessons which would uphold moral and spiritual values - Christian values.

Parliament decreed that a school's day should begin with an act of worship and that every child should be given at least one lesson of Religious Education every week. In many, many schools they don't do that now. What is happening to the moral life of this country? Where is our society going in 1989? What vision does it follow ... if any?

To whom do our children and young people look for guidance? To whom can they look?

What lead do they have? What are we making of the freedom which so many died to preserve for us?

It is the responsibility of the living to make meaningful the sacrifices of the dead.

A few years ago in a remote and unfrequented spot in Southern England a farmer came across an odd piece of wreckage. Closer examination convinced him that it was the wreckage of an aeroplane largely buried and overgrown. He told the authorities and the aircraft was dug out. It proved to be the wreckage of a Hurricane and in the cockpit there were still the remains of the hapless pilot. Engine and airframe numbers enabled them to identify the aircraft - and the lad who was flying it. His name was Colin Francis, and he had been shot down in the Battle of Britain. And so it was that in October

1984, more than forty-four years after he had been killed, he was buried with full military honours.

In an editorial item in one of our national Sunday newspapers the editor wrote this:

"We know so little about Pilot Officer Colin Francis. We know that he was an only son. We can guess how his father and mother, now long since dead, must have wept that day in August 1940, when they received the news that he was missing, believed killed. We know that his last flight in the Battle of Britain was also his first. Fresh from flying school, he was just 19 - barely old enough to shave. We also now know just how he died He was one of three Hurricane pilots who took on 75 German planes over the fields of Kent. The man who led the Hurricanes into battle was present when Colin Francis's body, found recently in the wreckage of his plane, was buried last Tuesday. He said, 'We went into the middle of them and I never saw him again. He was a damned fine kid, with lots of guts'." The editor ended his article: " Am I the only one this October Sunday morning who will find time to think not of the petty troubles which now surround us, but of a nineteen year old lad who died for all of us, such a long, long time ago?"

In the pages of many Squadron Memorial Books are written the names of lads who did not live to see their 20th Birthday.

Our text reads: "These all died in faith, not having received the promises, but having seen them and greeted them from afar"'.

"Seeing then that we are surrounded by so great a cloud of witnesses, let us run the race that is set before us, looking unto Jesus, the author and perfecter of our Faith".

We owe it to these people - to all whom we remember this day. So, let us run that race: Let us keep the FAITH. Let us stand for that which we know to be RIGHT and TRUE and GOOD

Looking unto Him who loved us, such that he gave his life for us. Who always stands beside us in our days of loneliness and suffering, And who has promised to those who endure to the end an inheritance which is imperishable, undefiled, laid up for us in heaven and which fadeth not away.

Amen

ACA Annual Service St Clement Dane's, 28th April 1991

In the name of the Father and of the Son and of the Holy Spirit, Amen. In the Epistle to the Hebrews, Chapter 11 and Verse 10, we read:

"For he looked for a city which hath foundations, whose Builder and Maker is God "

One of the key ideas to be found in the Epistle to the Hebrews is the idea that through all history there runs a purpose: History is not just a chain of random events strung together but also the unfolding of the plan of a larger scheme of things. The author of the Epistle illustrates his point by referring to a long list of names of heroes of the Hebrew nation who had performed so many prodigies of valour, and who had suffered so much persecution and abuse, but who had always had their eye on the future and on the benefit that future generations would reap from what they did.

One of the heroes he names is Abraham, who went out from the idolatrous city of Ur in Chaldaea: travelling out Westwards into the unknown, having no idea of what his own future would be, but having the sure faith that what he did was at the call of God - part of the purpose of God, and that his going would be for the blessing of his descendants. He went out into inhospitable, lonely and uncharted places as a nomad, looking not just for somewhere to pitch his moving tent for the night - not an encampment of goatskin shacks that would all be gone tomorrow - but a permanent city - unshakeable and immovable - an abiding city, a city that had foundations, whose Builder and Maker was God!

Last September we celebrated the 50th Anniversary of the Battle of Britain. We remembered 1940: we remembered when in the blue summer skies over the harvest fields of Southern England the pilots of Fighter Command with their weaving vapour trails wrote such a heroic page in the annals of the Royal Air Force. And we remembered how Bomber Command wrote another when the war was taken into the searchlight-swept night skies over Germany. We remembered how Hitler was driven to the decision that "Operation Sealion" would have to be indefinitely postponed! Our land was saved from invasion by the Nazis.

We never had the Gestapo in England with their middle-of-the-night knocks on the door "Come with us - at once!" No sudden arrests and disappearances. No trains of cattle-trucks packed with terrified men, women and children being taken to unknown sinister destinations. We did not have any of the refined barbarities of a "Protector" like Reinhardt Heydrich; no Auschwitz or Belsen or Buchenwalde.

Today we remember the men and women who lost their lives in saving us from such - and in preserving our freedom. And we should remember them because the debt we still owe them is enormous.

Since the Second World War there have been written further shining pages in other wars: in Korea, in the Falklands and, but a few weeks ago, in the Persian Gulf, where the courage and skill of our flying men won world-wide acclaim. Indeed, one report described their exploits as "inspirational". Another report said "They streaked across the desert into Iraq at camel's knee height' (Actually, that's fairly low!). "God Bless the Brits" "You've got to hand it to those guys!" (That surely must have been the BBC!)

We were proud of our Airmen - and rightly so. But such achievements are only won at a cost - a cost of injury and lives lost.

Mercifully in the Gulf War our casualties were very few but for those who did not come back, as for thousands before them, it meant the giving of their all. And to day when we remember those who have died in those various ways, we might ask ours ourselves the question "What would they have thought of what we have done with that freedom they died to preserve?"

What vision do we follow today? What City are we looking for in 1991?

To-day, as one reads the newspapers - any newspaper - one is compelled to admit that there are so many things in our modern world and in our society that are the very negation of what we stood for in the war.

A little time ago, at a Conference in Manchester, The Lord Chief Justice of England said:

"There has been a general lowering of standards at every stage of life and at every level." The 19th Century Reformers blamed crime or poverty and lack of medical care and lack of education. What will they blame now?

You don't need me to draw up a list of the things we read with dismay and disquiet in our newspapers: be it fraud and dishonesty in high places; the black economy; the drug scene; the dreadful violence; cruelty; the abuse of little children. And with our crime figures for the last year reaching an all-time high, how does our society compare with the sort of society we had in 1940?

It is not only parsons who are now saying that as a nation we have lost our direction; our sense of purpose. We are drifting and we are worried: for our children and our grandchildren. Where are we going next?

We sometimes feel as if we are in a labyrinth - and we've lost the thread. And when I look at the many unhappy things that have gone wrong in our society - and continue to go wrong - I remember some words of Jesus:

As he sat with his disciples in that upper room and shared with them that Last Supper there was great deliberation in all that he did - and great earnestness in all that he said. The hour had come: it was the eve of his death. He said that their relationship now was no longer that of master and servant but that of friends. And he said "Greater love hath no man than this - that he lay down his life for his friends".

This was the very thing that he himself was about to do. He broke the bread - and passed round the cup as symbols of his body and blood.

And then he said: "I am the Vine - you are the branches. As the branch cannot bear fruit of itself except it abide in the vine, so neither can you, except you abide in me. The moment that the branch is severed from the vine it begins to wilt and die - and it cannot bear fruit."

Let us not deceive ourselves. Christian morality is not something that can be achieved by any amount of clever legislation. Christian morality is the fruit of the Christian Faith - and you can't have the fruit without the plant that bears it. It is now the fashion to be amused at the simple faith of our forefathers, and their serious concern about trying to be good. They used words like "sin" and "sinners" - dreadful words. We demobilised them a long time ago. We now have much better words, which carefully avoid any idea of guilt. The big advantage with these new words is that whatever went wrong it wasn't really anybody's fault.

It is a very materialistic world in which we live. One would think that even success and achievement and fulfilment are only meant to be measured in pounds sterling. We are losing our hold on things spiritual. In a poll whose findings were published at Easter this year, it was declared that more than a third of Britons did not know why Easter was celebrated and even more did not know what happened on Good Friday.

What about the rising generation? There is a declared movement to remove the teaching of Christianity from our schools altogether. We are being cut off from our spiritual roots.

"As the branch cannot bear fruit except it abide in the vine, so neither can you except you abide in me." We wither as we are parted from the life-giving sustenance we receive from the vine. What has happened to our Christian witness?

OUR WAR is now ancient history and the aircraft we flew are museum pieces. But the question remains: What is the city we are looking for? What PURPOSE runs through the history we are making now?

When I look back at my time on the Squadron I remember my pals - so many of whom were killed. No doubt, you do the same. But, in particular, I remember my friends Paul Markides and Evan Price. They were friends - inseparable - and came from Rhodesia. Paul was 21: outrageously handsome - a bachelor, and having a great time. Evan was a few years older: 27, more reserved, and desperately in love with the beautiful young wife he had left behind in Rhodesia. They joined the RAF together, trained together, got their wings together, went to the same squadron, were in the same flight - became captains together . . . .

When I became a POW I lost touch with them and it was not until the war was over that I could try to trace them. I discovered that they had both been killed. Paul had been shot down over the continent on March 25th, 1942 and within an hour, Evan's damaged aircraft returning from the same Target (Essen) crashed in the Thames estuary with no survivors. Evan is buried on the Isle of Sheppey in Kent. Paul is buried hundreds of miles away - in Belgium - and both of them a long way from their homes in sunny Rhodesia and Evan never having seen the infant son which his beautiful young wife bore him.

And as I have stood by their graves I have asked myself -

> What was it that made them do what they did?
> What vision did they have in their minds that made them leave their homes and their families?
> What city were they looking for?
> And if they were to die in their quest, what did they hope they would have helped to achieve for those they left behind?

These were but two among many thousands.

Surely, it is the responsibility of the living to hold meaningful and keep meaningful the sacrifices of the dead.

How are we measuring up to that responsibility?

When we think of the world as it might be - as we want it to be - and the world as it is, we realise that we have a long way to go. But when we think of our "friends" who died in the war, and remember the sacrifices they made to save our nation and a Christian way of life, we must surely be filled with a sense of gratitude and of humility. But can we not, in honour of them and inspired by them, seek to regain our sense of purpose?

Let us not be ashamed of our faith. In the war our faith was our comfort. and inspiration. It was also our strength as a people. So, as we face the future, let us hold fast to our faith:

> Let us stand, when we know that we should stand.

16

Let us abide in the vine that is our spiritual life.

Let us seek to set before our young people the satisfying and abiding rewards, the happiness and the joy of a good and virtuous life - a Christian life.

Let us use our precious freedom, preserved for us at such cost, to build a nobler life.

In this our Annual Service of Commemoration and Dedication; in this beautiful house of God, now the Mother Church of the Royal Air Force; in this place risen from the ashes of devastation in War; in this place: hallowed by centuries of Christian witness and worship;

In this place: surrounded as we are by a host of unseen witnesses; let us re-dedicate ourselves to our quest: so that eventually, by God's grace, we may yet arrive at that city, that abiding city: the city that hath foundations, whose Builder and Maker is God.

Amen

50th Anniversary of D-Day Torquay Harbour, June 1994

In his play "King Henry V" Shakespeare tells the story of the expedition of Henry V and his army against France, and of the battle of Agincourt when his band of yeomen soldiers won an almost incredible victory against great odds. That was on St. Crispin's Day, 25th October 1415; and in the speech, which he made to his hard-pressed troops on the morning of the battle, the king is represented as saying: "Whoever fights with me to-day is my brother - however humble his station"

And he goes on to say:

> "He that shall live this day, and see old age,
> Will yearly on the vigil feast his neighbours
> And say, "Tomorrow is St. Crispian"
> Then he will strip his sleeve, and show his scars,
> And say "These wounds I had on Crispin's Day"
> I was there. I was one of them."

Well, the battle of Agincourt was a long time ago, and the whys and wherefores of King Henry's campaign are known only to Historians.

But to-day we are here assembled to recall another campaign in France: one on a vastly greater scale than Henry's - indeed, one involving the greatest invading force ever put together in the history of warfare; a force which was to make a titanic onslaught on the enemy by land and sea and in the air - and the whys and wherefores of that campaign we all remember very well indeed.

Most of Europe was held in the iron grip of Naziism; held in subjection and fear by the minions of Hitler and his evil hierarchy, whose agents were the SS and the Gestapo, and whose institutions included concentration camps such as Belsen and Buchenwalde, and extermination camps such as Auschwitz and Treblinka.

Such was the enemy, and this enemy was occupying a Europe which they had massively fortified with mile after mile of concrete and steel defences and heavy gun positions. To storm that fortress and set Europe free was the daunting objective of D-Day; and the forces which were to make that assault had been assembled from the armed forces of many nations welded into one mighty weapon: men not only from the British Isles but from America, Australia, Canada, New Zealand, Rhodesia, from countries occupied by the Germans, Poland, Holland, Czechoslovakia, the Free French, and many more.

But though this armada was on such an enormous scale, in spirit it was one with Henry's army. "Whoever fights alongside me to-day is my brother."

Today we shall all do our piece - we shall not shame the stock from which we are sprung. And in the years to come those of us who survive this battle will meet - and tell the tale, and show our wounds. (This was a much bigger thing than Henry's undertaking - but still we were a brotherhood).

And here we are: We are happy to be here; and we are proud, and rightly so, of the part we played; and we are proud of our comrades who fell in the fight.

In our celebrations let us not lose sight of the fact that of those who went into action on D-day there were many thousands who would lose their lives in the landing itself, and in the long months of fighting before VE Day. Their graves lie in long neat rows in so many cemeteries all over Europe. They are still visited by grieving widows and members of their families.

On this anniversary day we remember them, we salute them and we give thanks to God for the service they gave, for their courage and the brave deeds they performed, for their endurance, their suffering and their sacrifice. And we thank Almighty God for our deliverance, for our survival and the prevailing of our cause.

On the night of the 5th June 1944, all over the South of England people awoke, or, if they had not yet gone to bed, they stopped what they were doing and went outside to listen. The air throbbed with the beat of hundreds of aero-engines. They were well acquainted with the sound of bombers flying out and coming back from raids into enemy territory - but this was different. This was the greatest fleet of aircraft they had ever heard - the greatest fleet of aircraft anyone had ever heard - all flying to the South. People called to one another: "This is it!" This fleet of aircraft was matched by a comparable enormous fleet of ships: some 6000 ships and landing craft; stretching from the Thames to the Bristol Channel - and all these machines carrying men, paratroopers, sailors, airmen, merchant seamen, commandos, marines, soldiers, tank crews - and all fully armed. This was the invasion. From the Torbay area alone more than 200 ships sailed: many carrying men of the American 4th Infantry Division to Utah beach. Most of our British forces sailed from the Portsmouth area making for the Beaches code-named Gold and Sword.

For the people of Britain D-day came at the end of four long years of unremitting hard work, by day and night, by men and women, in all walks of life, to make good the terrible reverses suffered in 1940, when England had been on the very brink of defeat. Four years of air raids, and the blackout, and everything severely rationed.

When France collapsed in May 1940 our army had to be rescued from the beaches of Dunkirk: a rescue, which was effected by a flotilla of every kind of craft imaginable, ranging from pleasure paddle steamers to small motor boats.

But though we rescued the army, it had lost all its tanks and heavy guns and equipment. And the United Kingdom and its empire stood alone. The Battle of Britain fought in the summer skies over the harvest fields of Southern England was a defiant and desperate fight for survival.

But now in June 1944 after four more years of war, with our friends and allies by our side, we were ready. This was the casting of the dice - the crunch. We prayed for Victory. Oh yes; on D-day from New York it was reported that men and women coming off night-shift were going into churches on the way home to pray for the success of our enterprise. A daily paper threw out its leading article and printed in its place the Lord's Prayer. In St. Paul's Cathedral and Westminster Abbey and many other churches, people knelt and prayed for the war to end and for the safety of our men.

The war did not end overnight. We still had almost another year of bitter fighting to endure before the day of Victory dawned - VE Day - when there was singing and dancing in the streets and church bells rang in every steeple in the land. The war in Europe was over.

To-day, in gratitude and in humility we look back across 50 years to D-day and we may well ask ourselves what have we made of the freedom that we achieved at the cost of so much effort and suffering, and sacrifice. Have we built the sort of world for which our comrades died? Are we prepared to live for the ideals for which they gave their lives?

It is so easy to forget - so easy not to acknowledge the debt we owe - so easy to live in heedless ingratitude and to let our children grow up in ignorance of the things to which they owe so much. To day there are so many things in our world and in our society that fill us with disquiet and dismay - but there are also many things that give us hope. The bonds of friendship and comradeship forged in the war still abide; they don't break; they stay strong. The fellowship - the brotherhood - goes on.

So to-day as we pray for the peace of the world (and there are none more earnest in their prayers for peace than those who have themselves experienced the miseries and barbarities of war); as we pray for the day when all men shall "beat their swords into plough-shares"; the day when "nation shall speak peace unto nation - and not learn war any more"; could we not find in our renewed zeal and unity of spirit the strength to finish the job? So that not only may peace prevail in our lands but that justice and righteousness may adorn the liberty we won? Could we not this day re-dedicate ourselves to that quest?

May God give us grace to do so. That surely would be the crowning achievement of those noble ideals that we had in mind as we took to the air, or manned the ships, or shouldered our arms on D-day.

ACA Reunion Plymouth Pavilions, 1ˢᵗ October 1995

This morning for a few minutes I would like to draw your attention to what St Paul said to his friends from Ephesus as it is recorded in Acts 20, verse 35. He said: *"Remember the words of Jesus"*.

This year, 1995, we are celebrating the 50ᵗʰ anniversary of the ending of the war:

> 50 years since VE day and VJ day;
> 50 years since the lights went on again all over the world and
> Bluebirds took off in droves to fly over the White Cliffs of Dover.

If you were on operations during the war and had been given a Divine assurance that you would live to go home safe and sound at the end of the war, that would have been a blessing indeed; but if you had been further assured that you would live to see the 50ᵗʰ anniversaries of VE and VJ day, that would have been a benediction beyond the telling, when at the time it looked as if you would be lucky to reach the ripe old age of 22 or 23. But here we are, still in the land of the living, and once more sharing in the act of Remembrance.

It may well be that for some of us this will be our last National Reunion, and so it was that when I started to think about what I might preach about today I eventually found myself thinking about St Paul and his Christian friends in Ephesus.

In the spring of 58AD Paul was in Corinth and he planned to take the ship from there that would enable him to be in Jerusalem for the Feast of the Passover, our Easter time. When he discovered that his enemies had plotted to have him killed on the voyage, he changed his plans. He walked back Eastwards as far as Macedonia and there boarded a ship which would get him to Palestine so that he could be in Jerusalem for the Feast of Pentecost, seven weeks after the Passover.

This ship called at Miletus (a few miles south of Ephesus) and he arranged for his friends from Ephesus to meet him there. They came down and met him on the shore. It was a very moving affair, as we have read in the first Lesson. Paul told them that they would not be seeing his face again – nor did they. After his conversation with them, they all knelt down together and he prayed God to bless them; and it was with tears in their eyes that they saw him back to the ship, and waved him out of sight.

What was it that Paul said to them at that farewell meeting? Basically, he said three things, and these I commend to you.

FIRST, Paul told his friends to Remember. Remember the time that they had spent together, the experiences that they had shared – all the friends who had been part of the fellowship – people whose companionship had been an enrichment of their lives.

I am sure that all of us here have a great wealth of such memories, and it is very important that we do remember the things that happened in the war as we experienced them. One is reminded of Henry V's speech at Agincourt (as Shakespeare has it):

"This story shall the good man teach his son,
And Crispin Crispian shall ne'er go by
From this day to the ending of the world
But we in it shall be remembered.
We few, we happy few, we band of brothers."

It is very easy to forget; life moves on, and things change; but some things we cannot, as a nation, afford to forget.

A few weeks ago, we had the special spectacular parades which celebrated the 50th anniversary of VJ day. And we saw the surviving veterans of the war in the Far East marching so smartly to the music, wearing their berets and decorations and campaign medals with pride. When they were interviewed, nearly all of these men said how important it was that we remember those who suffered such barbarous cruel treatment as prisoners of the Japanese, and especially those who came to wretched ends in misery and squalor. They insisted that we must not allow their deaths to be politely dropped from the record, as if they were a mere trifle, not worth mentioning, or something better overlooked for political reasons or considerations of policy. That is not good enough – it is an affront.

The great events of the war are indelibly printed on our minds. We remember the collapse of France in 1940; the Battle of Britain; the Battle of the Atlantic; Pearl Harbour; Arnhem; D-day etc. We shall never forget them. But we must make sure that these things also stay in our children's history books.

Perhaps most of us gathered here particularly remember the Bomber Offensive against Germany. Isn't it amazing how clearly those days on the Squadron come back to us? Old aircrew remember the 101 things you had to do before you got the green light on the Aldis from the duty pilot and were waved off: to face heaven knows what hazards … thick cloud, fog, ice, headwinds, not to mention mechanical failure, fire, flak, fighters and the icy sea in the dark.

Ground crews remember dark cold nights waiting near the flight huts, waiting and listening for the sound of aircraft which were "overdue". The WAAFs remember being in the Ops Room anxiously counting in the aircraft as they returned; not just the aircraft, but also the lads who were in them, boyfriends, fiancés, husbands-to-be.

All gave of their best in service to the cause to which we, as a nation, were committed – the destruction and eradication of Naziism and all its monstrous evils. You don't need me to enumerate those. Was there ever a more Satanic piece of cynicism than the slogan over the gates which greeted newcomers to Auschwitz:

"ARBEIT MACHT FREI" ("Work makes you free!")

When eventually Auschwitz was overrun, they did not find a lot of free people, just a lot of unspeakable horrors, and Auschwitz was only one of a considerable number of such places.

There is quite a fashion today to rewrite the war, from some trendy, perverse viewpoint, to stand in moral judgement on those who fought in the war. Indeed, to denigrate and belittle their efforts, or to put out TV programmes, produced by Channel 4 'experts' from Ireland, presenting "a different point of view".

Our struggle to survive as a nation and our efforts to overthrow the Nazis called forth from almost everyone in the land the best and the noblest that was in them. There were so many deeds of valour, bravery and heroism, indeed of self-denial and self-sacrifice, deeds beyond number. We must remember this; remember our comrades who died in their thousands on battlefields in so many theatres of war, on the sea, under the sea, and in the air; over 55,000 in Bomber Command.

And we must remember not simply the events, but remember the spirit which motivated us in those days. One of the most moving examples of this must be the letter whish a young pilot, named Vivian Rosewarne, left to be sent to his mother, if he was reported "missing". He wrote:

> *Dearest Mother,*
>
> *If I am reported "missing", you must hope on for a month, but after the end of that time you must accept the fact that I have handed my task over to the extremely capable hands of my comrades of the Royal Air Force, as so many splendid fellows have already done.*
>
> *Though it will be difficult for you, you will disappoint me if you do not at least try to accept the facts dispassionately, for I shall have done my duty to the utmost of my ability. No man can do more, and no one calling himself a man can do less. Today we are faced with the greatest organised threat to Christianity and civilisation that the*

world has ever seen, and I count myself lucky and honoured to be the right age and fully trained to throw my full weight into the scale. For this I have to thank you.

You must not grieve for me, for if you really believe in religion and all that it entails, that would be hypocrisy. I have no fear of death, only a queer elation – I would have it no other way. The universe is so vast and so ageless that the life of one man can only be justified by the measure of his sacrifice.

I count myself fortunate in that I have seen the whole country and known men of every calling. But with the final test of war I consider my character fully developed. Thus at my early age my earthly mission is already fulfilled and I am prepared to die with just one regret, and one only, that I could not devote myself to making your declining years more happy by being with you: but you will live in peace and freedom, and I shall have directly contributed to that, so here again, my life will not have been in vain.

Your loving Son,

Vivian

Vivian Rosewarne, an only son, aged just 23, pilot of a Wellington, was shot down and killed at Dunkirk in May 1940.

It is the responsibility of the living to make meaningful and to keep meaningful the sacrifices of the dead. We must remember them and the things we shared with them.

The SECOND thing which Paul told his friends from Ephesus to remember was: to love one another. Christian love is not a sort of anaemic sentimentality, a soppy sort of thing. Jesus said: "Greater love hath no man than this: that a man lays down his life for his friends." There is nothing soppy about that, and I dare say that most of us know of instances of men who deliberately made the supreme sacrifice to save their friends. Like the pilot staying at the controls of a stricken aircraft to give his crew the chance to bale out; or the airman who clipped his own parachute chest pack on to another crew member whose own parachute pack had been destroyed; or Padre Pugh who, when HMS Anselm was torpedoed in the Southern Atlantic, insisted on being lowered on a rope to get down to the sick bay so that he could be with the wounded men lying there helpless in their beds, so that he could give them words of comfort as he went down with them.

Remember, says Paul, that the bonds which bound us together then, bind us still: the bonds of trust, reliance, loyalty and service. The bonds of a common faith: the bonds of Christian love.

Oh! That as a nation we could recapture the faith and vision of the war years! Our Reunions bear testimony to the fact that, for us at any rate, this feeling goes on; as Paul said in his letter to the Corinthians, Christian love "Abides". We have enjoyed a rich fellowship with one another. We know Christian love is not just for times of danger and deprivation and hardship. It stays with us always, and is at the centre of our times of happiness, joy, doing things together and sharing.

Remember that love goes on. Remember to love one another.

And the THIRD thing which Paul told his friends to remember was to *Remember the words of Jesus,* Remember how He said: " It is more blessed to give than to receive", and remember that that was not just something that He said, it was always that spirit of giving which motivated His every action. Jesus gave His all. His whole life was a constant outpouring of himself in love.

Jesus spoke as a man to men and women who were children of God, and so long as men remain men, and women remain women, the words of Jesus will be relevant. He speaks to us on our level: human beings in the midst of this transitory life. He knows what we are made of, and He knows our problems, and He knows what courage is all about.

The story of Jesus is the story of a man who died that we might live. He calls us to Himself as he called those who died on operations during the war, climbing "per ardua ad astra", climbing those difficult paths to the stars. And we have His promise: "I am with you always, in every situation, even unto the end of the world."

And now, if I may take one last leaf from Paul's book, I commend you to God; and I commend you to all things which speak of Jesus and his love for us; things which will support and comfort and strengthen you, and ensure for you a place among those who are His redeemed, both in this world, and in that place which He has gone to prepare for us.

God bless you all. Remember, remember the words of Jesus and His Grace be upon you all.

Amen

ACA Annual Service St. Clement Dane's, 27th April 1997

For a few minutes this morning I would like us to consider the words with which St Paul closes his second letter to the Corinthians:

In II Cor.13[13], we read: *"The Grace of our Lord Jesus Christ, and the Love of God, and the Fellowship of the Holy Spirit be with you all. Amen"*

When we think of the disciples of Jesus we nearly always think of them as we see them depicted in the stained glass windows of our churches and cathedrals: all very holy, very righteous and very other-worldly. I wonder if the original disciples would recognise themselves! Apart from Judas "Iscariot" (Judas the man from Kerioth, a place in Judea), and Matthew, the tax collector, the disciples of Jesus were hardy Galilean workingmen: fishermen, farmers, and peasants. These were the men Jesus called and it was the experience and the life they shared which knitted them together.

There were, to be sure, times of difficulty but there were also times of tremendous spiritual uplift - of wonder and amazement at this man Jesus. By his words and example he set before them a way of life that had an irresistible appeal. He set all human life in a context that transformed everything about it. He challenged them to lay hold more fully on their true status as children of God

And as they were drawn ever more closely to him, they were drawn ever more closely to one another; and the relationship of master and-disciple gave way to the fellowship of "friends" - reminiscent of Shakespeare's Henry V and his troops:

"We few, we happy few, we band of brothers".

That line appears in the memorial window of the airman's chapel in Westminster Abbey - and it is very apt.

I don't think that the feeling of fellowship was stronger in any arm of the services than it was among aircrew. I remember my time at 18 E.F.T.S in 1940 (at Fairoaks in Surrey) where I and a number of others were introduced to a whirring yellow and green aeronautic device known as the Tiger Moth. I think some of you will probably remember it! We were billeted in a very large fine country house, eight of us in the bedroom where I slept. I remember one dark night, after "lights out", one of our number (Bill Massey) came in late: he lit a candle and came across to my bed and said, "Vic, I think I am dying". "Oh no Bill, and you so young! Are you bleeding to death? It's not the dreaded Beri-Beri?" "No – Hunger! I don't think I shall make the morning. Do you have anything to eat in that cake tin that you keep in your locker?" (There was a gracious lady who used to send mc the occasional fruit loaf). "Well

26

Bill," I said, "The thing is I haven't got a knife". It was not a good answer! In a twinkling of an eye I was offered the choice of seven knives - all most kindly offered and backed by wide smiling faces. Hmm! ... So a good slice of this heavenly manna all round, and eaten to such sincere expletives as "Smashing! Super! Wizard!" until the cake tin lid was once more making a good airtight seal on about six crumbs and we all got back into bed - and none of us died of hunger during the night.

Looking back at that scene and remembering how many of those lads were to lay down their lives for their friends I find in it something almost sacramental.

It was the same with my pals in the prison camp. Now it can be told that I was an inmate of a nice selection of prison camps - one of a group of about 250 RAF prisoners who were moved around as a body. What a day it was in May 1945 when we were flown back to England in Lancasters - 25 to a Lanc. Then leave - we could not get home fast enough. And after some leave we went back to be sorted out - only a couple of days – immediate demob – delayed demob – hospital treatment - staying in the RAF - going home - travel warrants - to be off the next day. But that night no one went out of the camp: the mess was crowded. It suddenly hit us. This was it. The circle was about to be broken. Of my own inner circle who had been through so much together for some three and a half years, Jerry Poulton would be going home to Australia, Tazzie Thomas to Tasmania, Tom Barnet to Rhodesia, Geoff Allen to New Zealand, and Kennie Laing and Ike Hewitt to Canada. And this would be the last time we would all be together. But though this was the last time we would all be seeing one another, the fellowship would go on: that would never break.

When the disciples realised that the circle of their fellowship with Jesus was soon to be broken they were on their way to Jerusalem, and Jesus was striding on in front of them with such purpose and with such a look on his face that they were filled with deep foreboding. St Mark says, "As they followed, they were afraid..." Their fears were well grounded. They stayed in Bethany. A week before the Passover Feast Jesus rode into Jerusalem on a donkey - the original Palm Sunday. Four days later they sat down with Jesus at what was to be their Last Supper together; when Jesus broke and shared a small loaf of bread with them, and then a cup of wine. Then he prayed for them and they went out into the garden of Gethsemane: and within 24 hours he was dead and, in somebody else's grave, buried.

The disciples were appalled, unbelieving, stunned, shattered - overwhelmed with a sense of empty desolation. This was the end! BUT IT WASN'T. The

Gospel does not end there. Three amazing things happened: The Resurrection, the Ascension and the Day of Pentecost.

The risen Jesus was seen on Easter day by a number of people, including the disciples, in and around Jerusalem. He was seen by them again, and by many others, in other places over the next five or six weeks, until his repeated appearances built up in their minds the conviction that though they could not see him all the time, he always knew where they were, and could come to them, anywhere. He was still there – he was always there. That was an ongoing experience, until Ascension Day, when He appeared for one last time. He took them out on to the Mount of Olives, and he said to them, "I am with you always, even unto the end of the world." Then he raised his hands over them in blessing and a cloud (a common symbol of God throughout the whole of the Old Testament), a cloud, God, received him out of their sight. And they knew that they would never see him again with their mortal eyes.

That was it.

And then we have that verse in St Luke's account, which almost comes as a shock. *They returned to Jerusalem with great Joy!* Not plumbing the depths of misery and despair. No....JOY!

Glowing with the conviction that Christ was alive for evermore and that their fellowship with him and one another would go on and that neither the passage of time nor death itself could ever break it.

Our reading this morning, from St Paul's Epistle to the Romans, says exactly that.

The dimension of eternity, of God's eternal kingdom, is an integral part of the Christian message. If you try to cut out "eternity" and "heaven" and "all that sort of stuff" from the New Testament account of the teaching of Jesus, what you have left is not the Christian Gospel.

Jesus always addressed men and women as children of God: children of a loving Father Creator; children who had something of their Father in them; children whose transitory life here on earth was only part of the story. Jesus did not argue for this, he took it for granted and he used it as the foundation stone of his teaching. "In you, Father, we are one family in earth and heaven." And this family is bound together in the fellowship of the Holy Spirit: and you and I are in it: not by being plaster saints but as we have Christian love for one another. The Holy Spirit is the love which was in Jesus. And the Fellowship of the Holy Spirit is the fellowship of those who have this love for one another. That is the heart of the matter. The doctrine of the Fellowship of the Holy Spirit – like the belief in the Resurrection of Jesus - was not worked out as a desirable theological concept in a reasoned scheme of systematic theology. No, it sprang from men's experience of it. The fellowship was a reality: the fact, a real living bond. It was part of everyday life to be shared not just by the pious and privileged other-worldly, but by *all* who wished to be part of it: ordinary people like you and me.

I am sure that we could all tell stories of the gallant things that men did for their brothers-in-arms, in the war on land, or sea, or in the air, and the thing that motivated these brave deeds was not a set of rules of engagement: it was the personal bonds of mutual esteem and concern - and affection. It was a two-way thing. It was something from which you drew, and to which you gave in return. It was much more than being in the same service together: it was the fellowship.

In this place where we are assembled there are recorded in the memorial books around us the names of thousands of young men and women who came from all corners of the world who were part of that fellowship, - and the Christian Faith asserts that that fellowship did not end with their deaths.

Our fellowship with those who have reached the stars before us goes on, it abides.

So let us live by the faith that God is a living God, and that he made us for fellowship with himself, and with one another. "In you, O Father, we are one family in earth and heaven."

That is our FAITH. That is our COMFORT, our STRENGTH, and our INNER JOY.

The Fellowship of the Holy Spirit be with you all

Amen.

ACA Reunion Service Dundee, 5th October 1997

In HEBREWS 12.1 we read:

"Seeing then that we are compassed about with so great a cloud of witnesses, let us run the race that is set before us, looking unto Jesus, the author and perfecter of our faith."

One of the little conundrums that Bible scholars ask one another is: "Who wrote the Epistle to the Hebrews'" and after long learned discussion about possible authors the answer they arrive at is "We don't know".

But though we may not know who the author of this Epistle was, we certainly know what his purpose was in writing it. He was trying to get the Hebrew people of his time to lay hold more fully on their spiritual inheritance and to live by the faith which was their heritage - indeed, their birthright. To help him to do this he holds up to his readers, one by one, a whole company of heroes of the Hebrew faith, Abraham, Moses, David, Gideon, Barak, Samson, and many more - men and women - pointing out the daunting situations which they faced; the sufferings they endured: mockery, scourging, torture; sometimes having to live like hunted animals, in caves and in holes in the ground; and in many cases dying violent and shocking deaths: "stoned, sawn asunder, slain with the sword". And the writer goes on to claim that all these heroic things they did and all that they endured bore witness to the FAITH which sustained them, the faith which they had preserved and handed on, the faith which you have now inherited, he says, and whose fruits you now enjoy, the faith by which they lived, and for which they died. These heroes were "witnesses" and these were the ones who gave to the word "witness" a new meaning.

In the Greek of the New Testament the word "witness" and the word "martyr" are the same word. So, he says, consider the FIGHT they put up - and remember that it was their FAITH which gave them the power to do what they did.

When we look back to the years of the war, even after fifty plus years, it is not difficult to see the enormity of the tasks which faced our armed forces and the awesome dangers that went with them. It is very easy to forget what tremendous sacrifices people made in the war, and the selfless brave deeds that were done by ordinary people, drawn from all walks of life.

When in September 1939 Hitler invaded Poland and we declared war on Germany, it meant that everybody was now in the war and all had to make their personal contribution to the war effort, regardless of their military potential. As they went into the forces ordinary people put on uniforms they had never dreamt they would one day wear. As John Pudney has it in his poem: "Tom, Dick and Harry, plain names and numbers, Pilot, Observer, and Gunner..."

I remember that when I was at S.F.T.S. at Shawbury, to our C.G.I. (Chief Ground Instructor), a certain Squadron Leader, it was a source of endless dismay that he should be expected to turn out satisfactory new aircrew from the poor, inferior, shoddy material that was all that he was given to work with. It grieved him. Heaven knows he had tried. He was not a happy man! Indeed, he despaired of ever getting us to behave in a truly airman-like manner; and so he comforted himself by making our lives as onerous and miserable as he possibly could, and 1 suspect that there may have been one or two other C.G.I.s rather like him.

But the fact remains that in war countless brave and heroic things were done by ordinary people. The fight was fought unremittingly on land, on sea, in the depths of the sea, and in the air. And if that was the FIGHT, what can we say about the FAITH we had? What was it that kept us going?

In the war we all knew what we stood for. We believed that our cause was just, that we stood on the side of things which were morally right and good and true. It was not simply a struggle to preserve our freedom and liberty; it was also to establish a new and better society - a new and better world where man's spirit would be free to rise to higher and nobler things.

In the church services which I conducted in a nice selection of P.O.W. Camps in Germany during the war, when we sang "Onward Christian Soldiers" (as we often did) we sang it at the top of our voices. It was partly an act of defiance aimed at our German guards on the other side of the barbed wire whose only permitted rallying call was "Heil Hitler". It was also very much an act of our faith. In the war as a nation we narrowly survived the dangers of being invaded, and it was five more years before we arrived at VE and VJ Day. We kept our glorious freedom. The question is: what have we done with it? You do not need me to tell you how sadly and how widely the moral life of our society has declined since the end of the war. It has to be admitted that so many of our wonderful new "freedoms" have worked havoc on our society. What has happened to the institutions of Marriage, since the war; Family Life; Law and Order; Social Responsibility; Probity in Business; Integrity in Sport; The idea of Service?

What has happened to any pretence of Censorship of the vile, the perverted and degrading? How does what we have compare with the sort of society we were sure that we would build when the war was over?

That is the question - or if you like, what has happened to our FAITH?

You must have faith.

A few months ago one of my old Prisoner-of-War pals died, a New Zealand lad from Dunedin, Geoff Allen, pilot of a Manchester Bomber. When Geoff came to England in 1941 he already had an older brother in England, Ralph, also a pilot who had been awarded the D.F.M. He met Gwen, a girl who lived in Chingford. Geoff rated Gwen at about 15 or 16 out of 10! In December 1941, when Geoff was shot down over Brest and reported "missing", Ralph wrote to Gwen. His letter (which Geoff eventually showed me) contained this passage: "When (*not "if"*) my time comes, Gwen, please don't grieve for me. I'll welcome it. In fact I'm looking forward to it; I've lost all my pals and it'll be grand meeting them all again, as I know I shall, and, after all, I've had a good life".

At 23/24 years of age? With everything to live for? Less than a month after writing that letter Ralph was involved in an air crash and was killed.

As I have read that letter, something I have done many times, I find it very moving to contemplate his concern for others, his self-effacing bravery, and the simple certainty of his FAITH.

Jesus said "You must have faith, be it only as a grain of mustard seed, it will grow". FAITH is essential.

When Jesus came to his disciples in the upper room after his resurrection, the disciples were listening to Thomas who was saying, "1 don't believe it: I've heard all these stories... I won't believe it. Unless I can have personal proof". Jesus said "Thomas, feel my hand, feel my side. Don't be faithless, Thomas. Be a believer. Be in the fellowship. You must have faith. You can't live a full life without it" and Thomas knelt down and said "My Lord and my God"

Keep your faith. You need it to live by.

I suppose that many of the old operational airmen assembled here were once members of Bomber Command. Those who were in No.5 Group, or one of the neighbouring groups, will certainly remember one thing from their flying days: the sight of Lincoln Cathedral from the air. Some of you may perhaps think of other cathedrals or churches.

As one stands by Lincoln Cathedral and looks up at its great towers reaching up into the sky one can only wonder at the vision of those men who centuries ago conceived the idea of building an edifice on this awesome scale - to the GLORY OF GOD - and as one goes around inside where ever the eye falls one is reminded that only the very finest in materials and craftsmanship was good enough. The Cathedral was a material expression of men's FAITH. FAITH that God reigns as king in his universe and that all human life, all human endeavour and experience, are to be seen against this abiding and unchanging truth.

As you flew over the Cathedral going out on ops you felt reassured that it was there. That was part of England, and it was good and right, and no matter what happened to you, it would go on. For many, the sight of Lincoln Cathedral's three towers in the fading daylight was virtually their last and loveliest sight of England. The Cathedral was part of our inheritance: it belonged to us, to all of us, to the airmen flying over it and to the citizens of Lincoln down below hurrying home and putting up their blackouts.

And the inheritance was not just the stones and the stained glass and the carved oak: it was the FAITH which these embodied, the faith which made us all one, even with the men who built it. It was that faith which was, in our hour of need, our comfort, our support and our strength. Can we not, then, as a nation as we remember the dreadful price that was paid to preserve our freedom, resolve to stand by our FAITH with greater earnestness? Can we not pray, as one man once did to Jesus, "Lord. I believe; help me with my unbelief." "Seeing then that we are compassed about with so great a cloud of witnesses, let us run the race that is set before us, looking unto Jesus, the author and perfecter of our faith". And may we all at the last be able to say, as St Paul did in the last letter he wrote:

"I have fought the good fight, I have finished the race, I have kept the faith."
(II Tim 4,2)

Amen.

ACA Annual Service, St. Clement Dane's, 26th April 1998

In St. John's Gospel Ch. 15 and verse 15 we read the words of Jesus to his disciples at the last supper *"No longer do I call you servants... I have called you 'friends'"*.

As some of my hearers this morning already know, there was a time when I earned my living as a schoolmaster, teaching Latin and "Divinity", as it was then called. It was real old-fashioned Divinity! We actually read passages in the Bible, reading verses in turn round the class with the inevitable "howlers", of course. Such as "John the Baptist lived in the desert, and ate locusts and wild honey and wore a leather girdle round his lions!" "LOINS! Not lions, boy, loins!" "Please, Sir, what are loins?" (This followed by a careful explanation of what loins are.)

We discussed the moral teaching of the verses we read. We also wrote notes, as one boy did about the prodigal son, "When the younger son arrived in the far country he spent most of his money on wine and women and he wasted the rest! "

But the story which always produced a lively discussion was the one, the only, "miracle" which is recorded in all the four gospels: the feeding of the 5,000, when Jesus accepted those five little barley loaves (poor man's bread!) and the two small dried and salted fishes, said grace, and fed 5,000 people.

"What did Jesus do? Sir: did he miraculously multiply the five little loaves and fishes into enough food to feed the 5.000 people, breaking the laws of nature to do so? What about the old "Law of the Conservation of Matter" sir, which states that matter can neither be created nor destroyed". Did Jesus override that law? Or was it that when they saw Jesus breaking the loaves, other people handed to him their food supplies? Until everybody pitched in - all they had - and there was enough food for everybody?"

Let us suppose that we could have met someone as he came away from the feeding of the multitude. We would ask him "What happened?" "Where did the food come from to feed so many?" He might well have said: "1 don't know; after he had been talking to us we were asked to sit down in groups and he just kept on breaking and giving. And we all sat around like children in one great family; and he was our father feeding us. It was like God feeding mankind, his human family. So long as I live I will never forget what happened here today. We all shared the one meal. All kinds of people! I never dreamt that I would ever find myself sharing a meal with the likes of some of those that were there today. Some of those in my group - where did they come from? And yet we were all happy; we were glad to share, and with him there we felt that in him we were just one great fellowship. We'd got it right.

Somehow, we saw our lives in a new and wonderful context. I wouldn't have believed it. I'll never forget it!"

When I read that story of Jesus breaking the bread and distributing it I am always reminded of an experience I had as a guest of the Third Reich in Germany, in Stalag 383. I became very good friends with an Arab who had served in some Palestinian unit of the British Army. I think he was the only Arab in the camp. His name was Khalil Tawfik Najjar. He was a very good soldier though his rank had alternated fairly rapidly between sergeant and private, fortunately, at the time of his capture, sergeant. Apart from being an expert with all kind of weapons, and in all manner of martial arts, Khalil was a great gambler. I liked Khalil and in our conversations walking round the camp I used to point out to him that gambling often goes hand in hand with covetousness and that covetousness is listed among the seven "deadly" sins, and that gambling can be dangerously addictive. He used to listen very politely. But it has always been my experience that gamblers only listen to sermons about the evils of gambling when their gambling has brought them to a point where stark and total ruin is staring them in the face. That is when they listen and heartily agree with all that you say. But Khalil was not one of those. He was an outrageously successful gambler. Cigarettes were the usual camp currency, and on one occasion he won so many, I don't remember how many, boxes. He gave me a boxful, for me to spend like so much money. At which point I made the suggestion that we should celebrate our good fortune with a feast. We set a date, we bought in, we spared no expense, and eventually we sat down facing each other to a meal which, by P.O.W. standards, could only be compared with the Feast of Belshazzar in the Bible.

We were going to eat our fill. And I paused and said. "For what we are about to receive may the Lord make us truly thankful." Khalil looked at me and he grinned and said. "1 will break my bread and share my salt with you because you are my friend." And, though he did not know it, in that moment he carried me back nearly 2,000 years to that upper room in Jerusalem where Jesus sat down with his disciples for that Last Supper together. When he broke the bread and shared the cup and said, "1 call you no longer servants, but friends." And Khalil went on to explain that the sharing of bread and salt creates a bond.

> *If I sit down and share these with you, I have to be your friend.*
>
> *I have to stand by you, take your side, support you.*
>
> *And if I am not prepared to be your friend in this way I will not eat with you.*

So that is what it was all about: the shared meal was the bond of fellowship and mutual commitment.

When Jesus sat down with his disciples to eat the Last Supper together, when he broke the bread and said to his disciples "eat ye all of this" and "this do in remembrance of me" he was not simply asking them to do something to remember him by, he was deliberately establishing a bond of mutual commitment, he to them and they to him, binding himself to them and binding them to one another. And this bond was to stand apart from all limitations of time and space and the commitment was total.

It was in this context that Jesus uttered those words that have been inscribed on war memorials all over the world: *"Greater love hath no man than this, that a man lay down his life for his friends"*, and as he said those words he knew very well that within the next twenty-four hours this was precisely what he himself would do.

When we talk about the fellowship of friends we are not talking about something mythical or fictional, the sort of thing you read about in nice novels. Old servicemen, and perhaps none more so than old aircrew, know a good deal about fellowship. When we who have now reached maturity look back at the war years and remember the hazards that men faced as they went out on operational missions, is there anyone who cannot recall instances of men doing the most gallant, not to say desperately hazardous, things to save their friends who were in danger? I suspect that almost without exception those of you who flew in the war could tell stories of heroic things done by men - without hesitation - to help their friends, way beyond the call of duty.

I wonder how many instances there have been of pilots who have lost their lives staying at the controls of stricken aircraft, to give the rest of the crew a chance to bale out. The bonds of friendship which were forged then ignore the passage of time.

The world we live in today is very different from the world in which Jesus lived; and England in 1998 is a very different England from what it was in the war years, and it isn't all good news. There are too many things that cause us dismay and disquiet. We are now so "liberally-minded", so tolerant and accommodating of breaches of our old moral standards, that one wonders if there is any issue left which is not already hopelessly compromised. The argument that "Everybody does it, so it must be alright" is not good theology!

Let us not deceive ourselves: God is not mocked, as Jesus once tersely pointed out: "Men do not gather grapes of thorns or figs of thistles". What we sow is what we shall reap. Christian morality is the fruit of the Christian Faith, and you can't have the fruit without the plant that bears it. At the centre of the

Christian faith there stands this man Jesus Christ, and in less than two years time we shall be celebrating the 2,000th anniversary of his coming into the world. Jesus is the one moral teacher who not only taught people how to live; he lived a life of such moral goodness that he could simply say, "follow me".

When at the end of the sixth century of the Christian era that old Scythian monk Dionysius Exiguus divided history into B.C. and A.D. he was really asserting that the coming of Jesus into the world was the greatest event in human history. It was the crucial, definitive piece of the drama in the story of mankind. It was the pivot on which human history turned.

As the Te Deum puts it: Jesus "opened the kingdom of heaven to all believers", and He invited everybody to join this fellowship of "friends", the fellowship which endures, defying all limitations of time and space. On the day of his resurrection Jesus appeared to those friends at Emmaus, and revealed his abiding presence with us when, beyond death, he sat down with them to supper, and gave thanks, and broke the bread.

The bond between Christ and his friends is a timeless thing. It was not confined to the time of his life here on Earth. It is not confined to our transitory life here. It abides. It is part of God's eternal kingdom.

So let us be true to that company of 'friends': let us be true to our friends of the war years and to the noble ideals for which they fought.

May God give us grace to say, "0 God, make clean our hearts within us, and take not thy Holy Spirit from us. Lord help me to take my place in your family of "friends". I want you, O Lord, to break the bread of life to me. I want to be your man, or, I want to be your woman."

Amen

ACA Reunion at Gatwick, 5th October 1998

The book we call the Bible is actually a little library of books bound together in the one Volume: 66 Books, 39 in the Old Testament and 27 in the New Testament. The authors are a very mixed bunch and they wrote against a very wide range of historical backgrounds: War, Peace, Victory and Defeat, Plenty and Famine, Exile and Captivity, Persecution and Subjection. The time span covered by their efforts is about 1000 years and the books are of all kinds: History, Law, Poetry, Prophesy, and Philosophy. They vary widely in style, length (anything from one chapter to fifty), vocabulary, and literary merit. They are very different but they are all agreed on one thing: that the things that men do have a two-fold significance, their significance relative to the here and now and their significance viewed against the back-cloth of all human history, of eternity, of God.

One of the most common symbols for God, to be found in many churches, is the two Greek letters A and O - Alpha and Omega, the first and last letters of the Greek alphabet, the beginning and the end.

God had the first word, and he will have the last one. And the whole human drama fits in between these two. This was certainly the viewpoint of Jesus. He never argued about it. He took it as an accepted truth on which he could build his teaching.

Man is not just a fortuitous biological phenomenon. He is a child of God. As he said at his first temptation in the wilderness: "Man does not live by bread alone but by every word that proceedeth out of the mouth of God." Well, if that is the truth of the matter what has man to do about it? Well, said Jesus, the answer to that question can really be put quite simply:

You must love, acknowledge and revere the God who made you, who gave you life and being, and you must love your neighbour, your fellow man, as yourself. You must live as a child of God.

"Oh Vic", you might say, "that means I've got to be good." Yes, it does. "Oh Vic, trying to be good puts one under a terrible strain. Thou shalt not do this; or this; or that. It's like dieting .....you have to eat all the things you don't like! All the nice things in life are either illegal or immoral or fattening (or all three). Now don't get me wrong, Vic. I've nothing against goodness. I think we should have goodness and good people, like parsons and nuns and people who live in convents and monasteries and get up very early in the morning and say a lot of prayers. But I'm not in that bracket, Vic; it's just not my scene, man. I'm just not a religious man, Vic."

I've heard it all - one harrowing confession after another. But when I hear that kind of protestation I'm always reminded of that incident that we read about in our Gospel lesson... where Jesus, at the very beginning of his ministry was walking by the shore of the Sea of Galilee. He began to talk to the people there and it was not long before he had a crowd round him and this crowd pressed around him in such a way that Jesus got into Peter's boat and Peter pulled a few yards from the shore and Jesus continued to talk to the crowd from the boat.

Peter listened along with the rest. When he had finished his discourse, Jesus turned to Peter and said "And now, Peter, let us pull out into deep water and catch some fish". I think Peter must have greeted these words of Jesus with a wry smile and he said "We have been fishing all night and caught nothing there's nothing doing" ("and I should know if we are talking about fishing on the Sea of Galilee!") but he then added: "But we'll do as you say.... I will let down the net." ("We must do as the young teacher says.")

They took an enormous catch of fish, their nets were bursting. Peter looked at Jesus and he didn't just say "Well, that beats everything" - or its equivalent! He suddenly realised that he was in the presence of a something - a goodness - that he had never met before and all he could say was "You must forgive me, Jesus, I didn't know. I'm a fisherman, I'm a sinner, I'm not the sort of man you are looking for; I'm not a religious man.

And, Jesus just smiled at him and said-. "Oh Simon. You 'll see greater things than these".

Have you never felt yourself to be in the presence of the Divine? Looking at a sunset, or a harvest field, or a beautiful rose and catching its perfume? Or finding yourself touched by the sort of compassion that was in Jesus as he gave sight to a blind man, or sanity to a tormented lunatic? Or to hear the nicest sound I know, that of a little girl singing to herself unaware that anyone is listening?

"Earth is crammed with heaven and every bush aflame with God. But only those who see take off their shoes!"

Well, if you find it difficult to find God in this sort of way let me commend to you a poem which I learned when I was in Miss Gregson's class in the village school I attended as a boy. It is called "Abu Ben Adhem" (perhaps you remember it?). It tells this little story:

One night Abu Ben Adhem was sleeping peacefully in his bed and he woke up to find his bedroom filled with a soft warm light and when he sat up he saw the reason why. Sitting at a table in the comer of his room there was an angel writing in a book of gold. After a few moments he felt bold enough to ask "What are you writing?" "The names of those who love the Lord" "Is my name there?" "No." Abu Ben Adhem was somewhat dismayed to hear that, but perhaps not too surprised, because he was not what you would call a religious man. But the following night the angel appeared again and Abu Ben Adhem asked, "What are you writing now?" "I am writing the names of those with whom God is particularly pleased, because they love their fellow-men." "Is my name there?" "It is at the top of the page."

I often think of that poem when I remember the lads we flew with during the war. They were not saints. If you had suggested they were, you would have got a short and perhaps colourful reply. But they gave abundant proof that they loved their fellow men. You can't always judge people by their religious professions. Jesus knew that very well. He was certainly not deceived by the pretensions and posturing of some of the high churchmen of his time. His denunciations of the hypocrites and self-righteous are scathing in the extreme.

At the end of his Sermon on the Mount, he says "Not everyone that saith to me 'Lord... Lord...' shall enter the kingdom of heaven but he that doeth the will of my father which is in heaven.". The proof of the discipleship is in the doing. Real goodness is not a posture or the wearing of distinctive clothing. Real goodness is not a soppy, anaemic, gutless thing.

The good news that was in Jesus attracted not only the humbly honest of his time. It attracted the publicans, harlots, thieves; Simon the zealot - a political terrorist who became a disciple; the dying rebel on the cross "Lord remember me when you come in your kingdom".

To be a good man or a good woman is a noble calling. Why is it that in plays and sketches on TV, parsons are nearly always presented as great big silly simpering simpletons? Nice men speaking nice platitudes and not the slightest use, irrelevant, not really with us.

I ask myself that question when I think of Herbert Cecil Pugh. The Rev. Herbert Cecil Pugh was a Chaplain in the R.A.F. and in July 1941 he was on H.M.S. "Anselm" which sailed from Takoradi (West Africa) with 1300 passengers. Out in the Atlantic the ship was torpedoed. One torpedo hit a hold on C deck in such a way that it destroyed all escape routes from that part of the ship. The ship began to sink rapidly. Some minutes later someone said "Well, that's everybody off, apart from the poor wretches down in C deck".

When Padre Pugh heard that, he said, "Then I must get down to them". "You can't. What could you do? There's no possible way back." "Some were in the sick bay. There's a rope - lower me down on that rope." Reluctantly the officer took the rope and Padre Pugh was lowered down.

Afterwards, the officer said, "It was a sight I shall never forget". The water was already up to their knees as the men came to him. Padre Pugh knelt in the rising water to pray with them. "Well, lads, we'll all go together". The ship's officer managed to hurry to the ship's side and throw himself over the rail to safety. Moments later the ship had disappeared.

Padre Pugh's name shines on one of the memorial panels in St. Clement Danes Church listing the names of those who were awarded the George Cross. THOU SHALT LOVE THY NEIGHBOUR AS THYSELF. Surely, in what he then did, Padre Pugh was himself the embodiment of that love which will not let you go.

I have no doubt that you could all add other stories of men who gave their lives in deeds of great gallantry in the war. One of the ladies sitting at our table last night said to my wife: The medals I am wearing, I wear for my brother ... he was 17 when he joined the R.A.F. and just 19 when he was killed.

Jesus said *"Greater love hath no man than this ... that he lay down his life for his friends." "He that loseth his life for my sake and the gospels - the same shall save it."*

The Christian believer is part of the whole Christian story. He is part of its PAST, its PRESENT and its FUTURE and this truth is enshrined in the Christian Church's central rite - the Sacrament of the Holy Communion. UNION - ONENESS.

We are part of the PAST. As we recall that night when in that Upper Room Jesus broke the bread and handed round the cup, we are part of that great company; those who have been the good and faithful in his service, we are one with our parents, our grandparents, and war-time colleagues.

We are part of the PRESENT Church, as we acknowledge our ongoing fellowship and our love for one another, and

We are part of the FUTURE, as we look forward to the consummation of it all in that heavenly feast above, of which Jesus spoke.

We are all in it: all in that scheme Alpha to Omega. So let us be faithful to our calling and to one another.

> "Until with those who toiled and dreamed
> To build the Kingdom of his Grace,
> With those the world hath ne'er esteemed.
> With all the hosts of the redeemed,
> We see him face to face."

Amen

ACA Family Service Runnymede Memorial, 15th August 1999

(The memorial is dedicated to the memory of those service men and women who lost their lives in the war but who have no known grave.)

I will read a few lines taken from the last chapter of the book of Deuteronomy:

"And Moses went up from the plains of Moab into the mountain of Nebo, and the Lord showed him all the land of Gilead unto Dan.
And the Lord said unto him "This is the land which I swore unto Abraham, 'I will give this to thy seed.' I have caused thee to see it with thine eyes, but thou shalt not go thither".
So Moses died there in the land of Moab over against Beth-peor .
But no man knoweth of his sepulchre unto this day."

The Book of Deuteronomy is the last of what are called the five books of Moses. These are the first five books of the Bible, and they tell the story of how God called Moses from the burning bush to be the leader of the children of Israel who were then living as slaves in Egypt: how Moses stood before the Pharaoh and demanded that he should set these people free; how he led the Israelites out of captivity; and, after a journey across the wilderness of Sinai which took some forty years, how he brought them at last to the very borders of the promised land.

What a catalogue of difficulties and hardships and setbacks Moses endured to get the Israelites to this place! He was now an old man, completely exhausted by his labours, and in his heart he knew that he would not be going into Canaan. Moses made his way to the top of Mount Nebo and looked northwards and westwards. There it was, the Promised Land, the land "flowing with milk and honey"

Moses never came down from the mountain. He died up there, and the Bible says, "No man knoweth of his sepulchre unto this day". Moses had no known grave. But yet I think that, in a way, Moses died a happy man. He knew that, though he would not enter Canaan, the children of Israel surely would. For him, that was reward enough.

When we look back at the war years, after the collapse of France in May 1940, Great Britain and her Empire and Commonwealth allies stood alone. Our position was desperate. Churchill said:

"The Battle of France is over, the Battle of Britain is about to begin" and he added: "On the outcome of this Battle depends the future of Christian Civilisation" and he might have added "On the outcome of this war depends the issue of whether we preserve our freedom as a nation or become a subject state of Nazi Germany".

If we had failed at that point one shudders to contemplate what would have become of us as a nation, under the protectorate of people like Himmler and Heydrich.

The men and women that we remember today knew very well what the issues were, and knew very well what the odds were against survival. But they believed that our cause had to prevail no matter what the cost. They truly believed that they were fighting for the Right and that their efforts and their sacrifice would ensure a future that was peaceful and contented and morally good.

Like Moses on Mount Nebo they were looking over a promised land: a land of freedom and justice and human dignity; a land that they themselves would not enter, but which they would leave as a legacy to those who followed. How much did we owe them then? How much do we owe them still?

In a few days time we shall celebrate the 60th anniversary of the outbreak of the war and next year we shall celebrate the 55th anniversary of VE Day. The events of World War II will soon be passing beyond living memory.

The world we live in now is very different from the world of the war years and we cannot escape the question "What have we made of our survival? Of our victory in the war?"

There are so many things in our modern ""liberated" society that are a shame to mention, that are a sad betrayal of so many of the ideals for which men fought and died. We should never forget that the freedom we enjoy today was only won at a terrible price. We owe this freedom to those who counted not the cost of their service. Our shortfall we owe to ourselves.

The inscribed panels around us bear the names of thousands, men and women, dearly beloved sons, husbands, brothers, fathers, sweethearts, whose last resting places are known only to God. But the names we see around us will live!

The laurel that they bear is that when the great challenge came they were equal to it; they did not flinch or falter, but in their young manhood and young womanhood they went out to meet it, and gave their all, for the benefit of those that would follow.

That puts a lustre to their name that nothing - not even time - can ever take away.

ACA Commemorative Service St Clement Dane's, 29th April 2001

In the Epistle to the Hebrews Chapter II Verse 32 we read:

"...and what shall I more say? For the time would fail me to tell of Gideon, and of Barak and of Samson",

The Epistle to the Hebrews Chapter 11 is a sermon written by someone whose name we do not know, but who was very well versed in Hebrew lore. The subject of this sermon is FAITH: and after writing a few verses defining what faith is, the author goes on to cite instances of faith in action and he takes us through a Hall of Heroes of the Jewish Nation: Abraham, Isaac, Jacob, Joseph, Moses and others, pointing out the great hardships they endured, their terrible sufferings and martyrdoms, and the great things they achieved because of their faith. At the end of this list of names, he says ""and what shall I more say?" ...I would never have the time to tell you all about Gideon and Barak and Samson.

When we look back at the war years, if we were to take the Epistle to the Hebrews as our exemplar, we could certainly compile an impressive list of heroes who did prodigious things in the war, in all arms of the services. As for us, old airmen, we could soon make a list of air heroes - famous ones - but perhaps even more readily of men we knew personally, the lads with whom we flew, and record what they went through.

Today we are remembering, especially, those who became Prisoners of War. We remember those who were made prisoners in the war in Europe and North Africa and we remember those who became prisoners of the Japanese and who suffered with such fortitude the base indignities and barbaric cruelties that the Japanese heaped upon them.

Now that it can be told I can reveal that I became a Prisoner of War myself in January1942, starting off with a couple of nights in Amsterdam jail. One of the Prison Camps I was in as a guest of the Third Reich was Stalag 383 in Bavaria. where we were housed in wooden barracks, each hut accommodating 12 to 14 men. If I were to confine my list of heroes to the members of my barrack I would write "...and what shall I more say?" ...for the time would fail me if I told you all about Craig Hamilton, who had three of his Halifax engines shot out in various flak and fighter attacks before he and his crew had to jump for it; or of Kenny Laing, who crash landed his Spitfire in a daylight sweep over northern France; or of Tassie Thomas who managed to bale out of a blazing Manchester bomber during a daylight raid on the German Battleships Scharnhorst and Gneisenau at Brest;. ...Or of Ike Hewitt who managed to bale out of the same blazing bomber but, as he got out of the front hatch, his parachute had a great hole burnt in it, and as he fell he watched this

44

hole getting bigger and bigger as its edges smouldered away. He overtook other crew members who had baled out before him with no difficulty at all. Fortunately he fell into the sea. He nearly drowned bur survived: but his claim that he hit the seabed before he came up was challenged. It was pointed out that 16,000 feet is not really much more than three miles, and in any case he was repeatedly reminded, "If you can't take a joke you shouldn't have joined."

And I am sure I would run out of time if I told you all about Ray Heard and Rusty Gowing who were members of the crew of an old Bristol Bombay in North Africa which, on a paratrooper mission, flew over a German airfield in the desert. They actually watched the German fighters take off which came up and shot them down; ...or of Jerry Poulton who stayed in the cockpit of his stricken Hampden to help the rest of the crew to escape until his clothes were on fire; or of Geoff Allen who tried to take down with him on his parachute another crew member whose own chute had been destroyed. They managed to get out the aircraft together but when the parachute opened they were wrenched apart in mid-air.

The 12 prisoners in my barrack room came from the four corners of the world. We were four Englishmen, one from a neighbouring country called Scotland, two Canadians, one Tasmanian, one Australian, two New Zealanders and next door we had Tom Barnett from Rhodesia. But we were all welded into one great purposeful fellowship. There was no friction, no feeling of strangeness amongst us: there was a great deal of goodwill, and the fact that we came from homes thousands of miles apart was an enrichment of our fellowship.

When we got to Stalag IIIA at Luckenwalde we met our American counterparts: American airmen, POWs. This was the first time we had been able to talk to them: we had occasionally seen formations of American bombers flying over the Third Reich in broad daylight and in blatant disregard of Goering's declaration that no enemy bomber would ever be allowed to do that.

I was reminded about this feeling of oneness, a few days ago when I was looking at a book which was all about the Battle of Britain. There was a picture on the front cover of the book: a photograph of a squadron of fighter pilots answering the call to SCRAMBLE, and as they ran out to their Hurricanes a group of them were running hand in hand! That simple spontaneous, momentary, gesture said a lot. It was a real-life expression of Shakespeare's lines ..."We few, we happy few, we band of brothers."

But when I think of the lads I flew with during the war I cannot but think of my two friends Paul Markides and Evan Price, pilots from Rhodesia, from Bulawayo and Elizabethville. They were inseparable friends. They joined up together, got their wings together and were posted to the same squadron: No 83 at Scampton. Paul was outrageously handsome, aged 21 and single, having a great time. Evan was about 5 years older, rather more reserved, married and desperately in love with the beautiful young wife he had left behind in Rhodesia. I'm quite sure she was never out of his thoughts. When news came through that Evan's wife had produced a son we all went down to the Saracen's Head in Lincoln (now long since gone) to wet the baby's head.

Soon after that I was posted and it was not until the war was over that I was able to try to trace them. Both had been killed soon after my posting. Both captains, they were lost on the same raid to Essen in March 1942. Paul was shot down and perished with all his crew over the continent and within the hour, Evan, who managed to get his damaged aircraft back as far as the Thames Estuary, crashed there with no survivors. Paul is buried in Haverlee Cemetery in Belgium, hundreds of- miles from Evan who is buried in the Isle of Sheppey.

Evan never saw his beautiful young wife again, never saw his infant son. And as I have stood by their graves I have thought how easy it is to forget the appalling price that was paid to preserve our freedom, the freedom we still enjoy and which we so easily take for granted and so cheerfully abuse. And I have asked myself "what was it that moved them to do what they did, in that they volunteered to be trained as pilots and to take up the cause of a country thousands of miles away from the one in which they lived."

The writer of the Epistle to the Hebrews declares that the thing which bound the Old Testament Heroes together was their FAITH, Faith in their cause, and faith in the RIGHT which they believed their cause embodied.

In the war we were sure that in the struggle against Naziism we were fighting for the RIGHT.

Indeed that was our F AITH

It was our CAUSE

It was our STRENGTH

When we looked forward to the future it was tempting to think of the world fair as it might be: a world in which freedom was universal and where human society enjoyed the fruits of justice and righteousness; a world which reflected something of Isaiah's vision of "an earth that was filled with the Glory' of GOD as the waters cover the sea."

But it was not just a matter of Faith and Vision which motivated the heroes of the Old Testament and which was behind so many gallant things done in war. It was men's love of their fellow men; it was their readiness to serve, to serve and not to count the cost; it was "the love that lays upon the altar the dearest and best, the love that never falters, the love that pays the price, the love that makes undaunted the final sacrifice," as did Paul and Evan. Jesus said, 'Greater love hath no man than this, that a man lay down his life for his friends", the very" thing that he himself was about to do,

And what shall I more say? ...As we look back at what we achieved with our allies in the war years, in mutual esteem and in unity of purpose ...can we not find inspiration as we face the future ...as a people and as a church, to have FAITH and stand by it, to have that VISION and that CHRISTIAN LOVE?

Can we not take heart as we move into the Third Millennium of the Christian era - to strive for the coming of God's kingdom in all its fullness? Let us not lose sight of that vision. We need it. Following his vision of that time when God's will shall be done on earth as it is in heaven, the hymn writer John Greenleaf Whittier wrote these lines:

> Then shall all shackles fall: the stormy clamour
>
> Of wild war music o'er the earth shall cease,
>
> Love shall tread out the baleful fire of anger,
>
> And in its ashes plant the tree of PEACE.

The Grace of our Lord Jesus Christ be with you all.

Amen